MARSHALL FAULK

Rushing to Glory

by
Rob Rains

SPORTS PUBLISHING INC.
www.SportsPublishingInc.com

Production manager: Susan M. McKinney
Production coordinator: Erin J. Sands
Series editor: Rob Rains
Cover design: Scot Muncaster/Todd Lauer
Photo coordinator: Claudia Mitroi
Photos: AP/Wide World Photos, Joe Robbins and Brian Spurlock, San Diego
State University

ISBN: 1-58261-191-2
Library of Congress Catalog Card Number: 99-68613

SPORTS PUBLISHING INC.
SportsPublishingInc.com

Printed in the United States.

Contents

Marshall scores a touchdown as teammate Az-Zahir Hakim celebrates. (AP/Wide World Photos)

CHAPTER ONE

A New Start

In the days before the 1999 NFL draft, the St. Louis Rams were desperate to add a quality running back to their team. There was talk they would try to move up in the draft to take Ricky Williams, the Heisman Trophy winner from the University of Texas.

There were critics who questioned the plan. After all, this was a franchise that thought Lawrence Phillips was the answer to its rushing problems a few years ago.

John Shaw, president of the St. Louis Rams, looks on while running back Marshall Faulk signs his contract. (AP/Wide World Photos)

As they were exploring the options and deciding what to do, a new opportunity presented itself to the Rams. The Indianapolis Colts were willing to trade three-time Pro Bowler Marshall Faulk, one of the best running backs in the NFL the last five years.

It didn't take Coach Dick Vermeil and the Rams very long to say yes. They traded a second- and fifth-round pick in the draft to the Colts for the 26-year-old Marshall, who gained more all-purpose yardage in 1998 than any player in the NFL.

Marshall didn't care about the reasons the Colts decided to trade him. He wanted to concentrate on where he was going, and what he could do to help turn the Rams into a playoff team.

With the Colts, Marshall had started 76 of a possible 80 games, handled 34 percent of the offensive plays, accounted for 33 percent of the total

Marshall looks for the ball during passing drills at Rams Park, the team's training facility in St. Louis. (AP/Wide World Photos)

offense and scored 51 of the team's 148 offensive touchdowns.

He wants to be just as effective with the Rams, who have not qualified for the playoffs since the team moved to St. Louis from Los Angeles five seasons ago. Marshall wants to lead the team to that new level of success.

"My biggest thing in life is never to be a follower and always be a leader," Marshall says. "It's important for kids to remember that. Sometimes it means not listening to your friends. Sometimes it means having to make decisions on your own. Whether it's good or bad, if you make the decision on your own it's easier to live with them and deal with the consequences."

Time will tell whether the Rams or Colts made a good decision by agreeing to the trade. Marshall is betting on the Rams.

Although Marshall was disappointed when he was traded, he looks forward to playing with the Rams. (Joe Robbins)

"Two years from now we could be playing each other in the Super Bowl," Marshall says. "That would be great."

Reaching the Super Bowl would be the highlight of Marshall's life, a reward not only for himself but for all of the people who helped make certain that dream didn't die before he was able to even have a chance to make it come true.

Growing up in a tough neighborhood helped prepare Marshall for football. (AP/Wide World Photos)

Childhood

Marshall grew up in a tough neighborhood in New Orleans, only he and his friends didn't know it was tough. It was the only life they knew, and they thought it was the same kind of life everybody lived—except on television, and as Marshall said, "who believes what they see on TV?"

Marshall lived in a section of town known as the Desire Housing Project, a series of four apartments in a building, an area where violence and drugs were everyday occurrences. Marshall saw all of the problems, but somehow they seemed not to bother him.

"All I knew was that I had clothes on my back, shoes on my feet, food to eat and a roof over my head," Marshall said.

Marshall saw the problems of the neighborhood. He had a gun pulled on him and often saw one pulled on his friends. "Kids would be out playing wearing their new Christmas jacket or shoes, and somebody didn't get something," he says. "You were taken for money or clothes. It happened to me, it happened to friends of mine."

He saw people get shot in real life, not just on television. He saw drugs, and he had friends whose lives were ruined or ended by them. He saw kids drop out of school and begin living on the streets. It could have easily happened to Marshall, too, as it did to many in the neighborhood where the average yearly income was only $7,000.

One of the reasons Marshall was able to overcome the odds and make it out of the neighborhood was the support of his family. He was the sixth son of Cecile and Roosevelt Faulk. Even though his parents divorced when he was four, Marshall still knew they both loved him and were supportive of him. His mother worked several jobs providing for him and his brothers, including working as a cook in a department store and as a housekeeper. Marshall often spent the summers with his father, who was a truckdriver.

All of his brothers had played sports when they were young, but none took it as seriously as Marshall, who first began playing football when he was seven years old.

Knowing he had to answer to his parents, and also to his older brothers, was one of the reasons

Marshall runs off the field after making a play.
(Joe Robbins)

Marshall was able to keep himself out of trouble.

"I just didn't want to answer to those people," Marshall said. "I had friends who got mixed up in it. I was an average kid. I had some tough times, doing some bad stuff."

Marshall had some problems in school, getting kicked out of three elementary schools for different incidents. One time in the fourth grade he got mad and punched a girl in the mouth. She had accused Marshall—falsely, he says—of cheating.

When he and his friends would be standing on a street corner and a police car pulled up, they would run. Somebody in the group had probably done something wrong, Marshall says, such as having stolen something from a store, most likely, or thrown a rock through a window. Marshall says they were running just for fun.

"I think they enjoyed chasing us just for the exercise," Marshall says.

Despite knowing the problems he would face at home if he had gotten himself in more serious trouble, Marshall was faced with a choice. He could concentrate on sports—which meant he had to concentrate on doing well in school—or he could give up on both. He was about to enter high school when it clicked for him that his schoolwork had a lot to do with success in athletics.

"You can take every little kid, and regardless of what he's been told, and even as an adult, you want to find out things for yourself," Marshall says. "There's no experience better than self experience. It's hard sometimes to believe what people tell you. Sometimes you have to find out the hard way."

Marshall says his mother never told him he had to stay in school, but she made it clear that if he decided to stop going to school, he would have to get a job.

"My mom raised me differently than my brothers," Marshall said. "She really went hard at them, made them go to school. She gave me the options. She told me if I didn't want to go to school and didn't want to get an education, to do better for myself, then I could go to work and get a job. She told me that if I didn't want to go to school, then I had to go to work, 'You can't live in my house for free,' she said. I didn't want to work. I wanted to be a little kid still.

"When that happened, it changed my attitude because I wasn't going to school for my mother, I was going to school for me. I was going to school because I wanted to, and I wanted to excel. When I started looking at it that way, it made it easier to excel."

Marshall was taught another tough lesson about the relationship between academics and athletics when he was in the seventh grade. He had played

Marshall walks the tightrope on the Colts sideline.
(AP/Wide World Photos)

football in the neighborhood for several years and had grown to love the sport. He was looking forward to competing on a new level in middle school, but the school required all players to pass a physical examination before they would be allowed on the team.

A clinic in the area set aside one day to provide free physicals for the team members. It was the only day they were provided, and to get a private physician to perform a physical cost between $30 and $40. On that specific day, Marshall got in trouble with a new home room teacher and she ordered him to return to her room for detention after school.

Marshall missed getting the physical, and because his family couldn't afford the cost of a private physical, he had to miss that football season.

"I had to sit the year out, and that's when I realized how much I missed football and how much I liked it," he said.

Marshall sits on the field after a pass was intercepted.
(AP/Wide World Photos)

Marshall was about to meet a man who would make certain he didn't miss the opportunity to play football again.

Marshall's high school football coach had a great impact on his life. (San Diego State University)

High School

Wayne Reese was the football coach at Carver High School, and the type of person who could command and receive respect. A former Tennessee State halfback, Reese has been a coach and a physical education teacher since 1969. When he first met Marshall, he knew he was meeting someone special.

Even though he was in the eighth grade, Marshall worked out with the varsity. When Carver was leading Cohen High School in its homecoming game 33-0 with only seconds remaining, Reese allowed Marshall to enter the game to make his high school debut.

The quarterback threw a screen pass to Marshall, and he turned it into a 30-yard touchdown. Even after a great collegiate career and success in the pros, Marshall considers that touchdown one of the most important in his career.

"It was the most awesome moment I've ever had," Marshall says. "It was fun."

Even before he became a prep star at Carver, scoring touchdowns had come easily for Marshall. Whether he was playing organized football in the Recreation Department League or just playing with other kids in the neighborhood, any time his team needed to score, they got the ball into Marshall's hands.

The coaches on his early youth league teams

also played a role in his development and success, Marshall said.

"Coach Chris, he was my Little League coach, he helped me out a lot," Marshall says. "Coach Sampson was my coach at St. Rock. He taught me there were other people on the team and that I didn't always have to get the ball. Growing up, I always got the ball. I had to learn how to play with other people because there were other guys who were good too."

Those lessons were reinforced by Coach Reese, who took a special interest in Marshall's progress. By his sophomore year, Marshall not only was playing running back, but was seeing more action at other positions as well. By the time he was a senior, Marshall was also playing quarterback, wide receiver, defensive back, returning kicks and punts, kicking off and punting.

Marshall's coach was the first to mention college as an option. (AP/Wide World Photos)

"Coach Reese had a lot to do with teaching me the game," Marshall said. "He taught me that if I was going to play the game I had to love it. He taught me to understand the game, to know the game, not just play it. He made me know what I was doing, and also why I was doing it."

Coach Reese demanded discipline on his team. He wanted to make certain his players didn't run into problems off the field, so he tried to keep them as active as possible. He insisted they play other sports during the non-football season, and that included running track.

Marshall did not want to compete in track, but Coach Reese told him that if he didn't run track, he wouldn't be allowed to play football.

"He sat me down and told me the opportunities that were out there," Marshall said. "He was the first one that ever mentioned college to me. None of my brothers went to college, but he told me about the mistakes that a lot of people had made, and how it was up to me to not make them."

When he knew he had to run on the track team, Marshall was determined to do it well. He helped make Carver's teams in the sprint relays among the best in the city and state.

"By doing a lot of stuff like that he taught me a lot of lessons," Marshall said. "He taught me about how you have to make sacrifices to get where you want to go. I had to sacrifice my summers practicing for football and my springs running track."

Coach Reese knew that he was working in a neighborhood where there were many distractions and where even the most focused kids, like Marshall, could get into trouble very easily. He also knew the kids needed to strive to do well in school, and he tried to organize activities to help them do just that.

"When I first met him, he had a major attitude problem," Reese once said about Marshall. "He was a basic Upper Ninth Ward thug. Of course, you have to have that attitude to survive where he came from.

"We had to turn that attitude around, and as soon as he did, he began to excel at everything. Not just on the football field, but also in class. If you told him doing something was going to help him get ahead, you could bet that he was going to do it. On the field, he would work hard, play hard, carry the team—I don't know if I've ever seen anyone work so hard."

One of the ways Reese tried to help Marshall and the other players was to schedule an extra practice each day at 7 a.m. That accomplished two goals. By getting the players involved in the early-morning practice, he made them eligible for the school breakfast program, which assured that they would have a good healthy breakfast at the start of each day.

Marshall worked very hard in school to stay out of trouble.
(Brian Spurlock)

Having the kids at practice and breakfast also assured that they would be there for the start of classes, keeping them in school and making it harder for them to cut class.

"That's how he made sure you were in school," Marshall said.

Marshall even added weekends to his workout routine. Coach Reese would give him and other students the key to the weight room, so they could go in and lift weights and play basketball in the gym instead of just hanging out on the streets.

Marshall began receiving letters from colleges during his junior year, and he and Coach Reese talked about the factors he would have to consider in picking a college. First, he had to pass the ACT test to make certain he would be eligible to attend the college of his choice, Reese said.

The test was hard for Marshall, and the first time he took it, he didn't pass. After taking some extra classes designed to help him prepare for the test, he took it again as a senior and passed.

Marshall had other things on his mind during his senior year as well. Before the year began, his mother was ill and decided to move in with her sister while she was recovering. Marshall was not able to stay home by himself, but his aunt lived in a different part of New Orleans and if he moved that meant he would have to leave his friends and transfer to a different high school for his senior year.

Marshall had a friend, Mark Bruno, who lived across the street from Carver. Bruno's mom agreed to let Marshall move into their home for his senior year so he could continue to go to school at Carver.

Bruno looks back on those years now and understands why Marshall became a success.

"God had to do it, because that dude, he didn't do anything bad,'

Bruno told the *San Diego Union-Tribune*. "We could have sold drugs and all of that, but he didn't do that. It was like God put him down here to do this.

"He used to stay home and study. I'd say, "C'mon man, let's go and play ball." He'd say, "Wait until I finish." He boosted me. My grades went up one point my senior year."

Marshall's hard work both athletically and academically paid off, and one of the people who was happy to see it was Coach Reese.

"I believe this kid had his mind set on what he wanted to do by grade school," Reese said.

During his senior year, Marshall went to work at Carver, helping in the boiler room and on the janitorial staff.

"I got the heaters and the air conditioners going," Marshall said. "I swept the floors and picked

Marshall eludes an opponent for a touchdown during the first half at t
Louisiana Superdome. (AP/Wide World Photos)

up paper and stuff like that. I made about $60 a week, which was pretty good money back then. It was my first job, and it taught me about money and responsibility."

Lindsey Moore, the principal at Carver, joins Reese in praising Marshall for what he has accomplished.

"What a lot of people don't know, is that it was football and athletics that kept that young man straight," Moore told the *Union-Tribune.* "If he didn't have anything else to do, Marshall could have been just as good a criminal as he is an athlete now. He could have gone either way."

As Marshall completed his senior season and the letters and calls from college coaches continued to pour in, he had some decisions to make. He first had to decide which schools he wanted to visit, and then ultimately, make a choice about where he wanted to go to school.

*Marshall dives in for a touchdown against the Bengals.
(AP/Wide World Photos)*

Many of the big-time programs that contacted Marshall were interested in him as a defensive back, despite the fact he had rushed for more than 1,800 yards during his combined junior and senior seasons. While he liked playing defensive back, Marshall loved being a running back. One of the first decisions he made was that was the position he wanted to play in college.

He also decided two other things—he wanted to go away to school, thinking it would decrease the amount of distractions. He wouldn't be coming home so often, which would keep him from running the risk of hooking up with his old friends and deciding not to go back to school. He also decided he wanted to go to school in a city where he could make some business contacts so that if football didn't work out, he could use his connections to get a job and begin working and living in a city that he liked.

Marshall really wanted the chance to play as a running back in college. (San Diego State University)

"I sat down and talked to my mom, and she said, "You make the decision on what is best for you," Marshall said. "She said, "You're going to have to live with it. Whatever you do, I'm going to be behind you all the way.""

Marshall decided to take his five official recruiting visits to Miami, Nebraska, Texas A & M, LSU and San Diego State.

There was one more complication. The night before he was to leave on the trip to San Diego, his father died. He had been battling throat cancer for several months.

Marshall didn't know what to do. He knew he couldn't decide whether to attend San Diego State without taking a trip there to see what it was like, and this was the only weekend he could go before the signing date. Yet he also did not want to be disrespectful toward his father's memory.

"I talked to my mom and Coach Reese, and they both told me to show up and pay my respects and then get on the plane. They told me, "This decision is going to affect you the rest of your life. I think it really kind of helped me deal with my father's passing. I had other things on my mind, and I didn't really get the chance to grieve."

Marshall had a difficult time getting to San Diego. He was making the trip with Curtis Johnson, the Aztecs' receivers coach who was from New Orleans. They were fogged in at the New Orleans airport for four hours. When they landed in Houston, they were fogged in again. They finally made it to Dallas, then had to switch flights. They finally made it to San Diego about 10 hours late.

"I remember being in the coaches' office and having some of the other coaches say, 'You won't ever get that kid. He's already had a bad trip. He doesn't want to hear anything from us,'" Johnson said.

Marshall enjoyed his visit, however, and returned home ready to decide which college to pick.

Because of his 4.3 speed in the 40-yard dash, he was receiving a lot of interest from coaches who envisioned him becoming an All-America defensive back. Still, his love of running back was weighing on his mind as the signing date approached and the calls from Miami, Nebraska and the other schools came in.

"Coach kept telling me I was going to have to talk to those people pretty soon," Marshall said. "He said, 'Tell me what you want to do.' I said, 'Coach, I want to play running back. Whoever comes up and offers me the chance to play running back is where I'm going.'"

It was only a day or two later when Johnson called, asking Marshall what he thought of his visit to San Diego State, had he made up his mind, etc. He also told Marshall what he wanted to hear– they

Marshall decided on San Diego State.
(San Diego State University)

wanted him to come in as a running back.

Marshall made up his mind—he was going to San Diego State, even though he could easily have picked a more traditional football power.

"The fact the school didn't have a national reputation didn't matter to me," Marshall said. "If you're good, you're good. I didn't know how good I was or how good I was going to be."

He, and the rest of the country, was about to find that out.

Marshall had to compete for a position against two other players. (San Diego State University)

CHAPTER FOUR

Becoming a Star

The San Diego State coaches told Marshall he was one of five freshman running backs they were adding to the team. One of their veteran backs had to quit school to go to work to support his family, so that left the team with only two returning backs, both juniors.

"Curtis told me, 'If you feel like you're the guy, you have to beat them out.' That's what I set my mind to do," Marshall said.

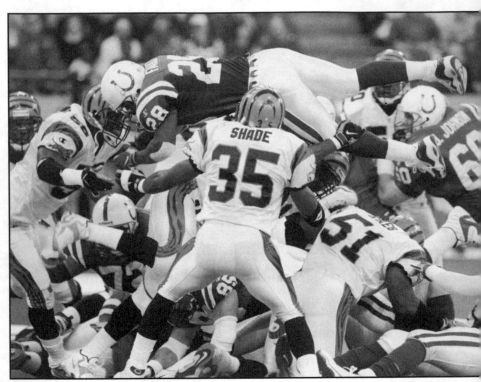

Marshall dives over the Cincinnati Bengals defense for a touchdown.
(AP/Wide World Photos)

When practice began, Marshall found out he had two weeks to show the coaches what he could do or they were planning to red-shirt him. That meant he would not play as a freshman, but would have an extra year of eligibility added.

In his first scrimmage, in August 1991, the coaches could tell his speed. Thoughts of red-shirting him were dropped.

In the first game of his collegiate career, against Long Beach State, Marshall was in the starting lineup and scored his first career touchdown. He felt good about his accomplishments, but not even his most optimistic fan could predict what was to come in his second game, the next week against the University of Pacific.

Marshall didn't start the game and didn't play until about four minutes remained in the first quarter. Nonetheless, he set an NCAA record, since broken, by rushing for 386 yards and seven touchdowns

Marshall always made a big impression in his debuts.
(AP/Wide World Photos)

on 37 carries. Suddenly, his picture was in newspapers and he was being talked about on all of the network television shows.

"I was out there having fun, just like I do now," Marshall said.

Marshall also was running to prove a point, however. He thought about all of the coaches who had tried to recruit him as a defensive back, and was running to show them he could too play and succeed as a running back in college.

Against Hawaii, he rushed for 214 yards and scored five touchdowns. Against Brigham Young, Marshall ran for 118 yards and scored twice in a 52-52 tie.

"The thing I remember most is how well he caught the ball," said BYU Coach LaVell Edwards. "You could tell he was a great runner. I remember watching their UCLA game (San Diego State lost 37-12). They got pounded, and I don't think

Marshall got a lot of yards (79). But when he got hit, I remember he always fell forward. I remember thinking that, for a young kid, he's relentless."

In the final game of the year against undefeated Miami, one of the schools that wanted him to play defense, Marshall rushed for 154 yards and two touchdowns. It was the most rushing yards the Hurricanes had surrendered in four years. He thinks they got the message.

By the end of the year, Marshall's name was showing up on various All-America teams. He rushed for 1,429 yards and became the first freshman in history to lead the country in rushing (158.8 yards per game) and scoring (15.6 points per game). He rushed for 21 touchdowns and caught passes for two more scores. He finished ninth in the voting for the Heisman Trophy, the second highest finish ever by a freshman (Herschel Walker was third in 1980).

He was only the third freshman ever to be named a first-team All-America by the Associated Press, joining Walker and Tony Dorsett. He tied Emmitt Smith for the earliest game for a freshman to reach the 1,000-yard mark, doing it in his seventh game of the year. In all, he broke or tied 13 NCAA records—and, almost as an afterthought, he missed three games because of two broken ribs and a punctured lung.

The success brought with it the expected media hype as Marshall began his sophomore season, with pre-season predictions listing him as a strong candidate to win the Heisman Trophy, awarded each year by the Downtown Athletic Club in New York to the player judged to be the best in college football.

Marshall tried not to get caught up in that talk, but it was hard. It also was hard because he was still a young player, learning what he needed to do to

Marshall led the nation in rushing as both a freshman and sophomore at San Diego State. (San Diego State University)

be successful and what it took to make the team successful.

"I always felt like I had to have the ball," Marshall said. "If we were going to run the ball 40 times I wanted all 40 carries. Sometimes I got all 40. I wouldn't come out of the game. I got hurt like that. Now I know I've got to come out of the game."

Marshall's performance as a sophomore was even better than his freshman year. Against Southern Cal, he rushed for 220 yards and three touchdowns. Against BYU again, he gained 299 yards and scored three touchdowns. He torched Hawaii again for 300 yards and four touchdowns.

"I've been here 16 years, and played against five Heisman winners," said Rainbows' coach Bob Wagner. "George Rogers, Ty Detmer, Marcus Allen, Charles White and Mike Rozier. I thought Faulk was a heck of a lot better than all of those."

Marshall finished the year with 1,630 rushing yards. He became the fifth player in NCAA history to lead the country in rushing in both his freshman and sophomore years, and the first to do it since Cornell's Ed Marinaro in 1970-71.

"When I saw the maturity level and understanding of the game that Marshall has, I would have sworn he was a fifth-year senior, not a freshman," Aztecs assistant coach Sean Payton said of his first encounter with Marshall. "The questions he asks are always the right ones, and his knowledge of the game is unbelievable. I don't know where it came from. He has the overall understanding of football that you want a quarterback to have, but a running back doesn't usually ever worry about. It's a big reason for his success."

Marshall's success made him one of the favorites as he went to New York to attend the Heisman ceremony. The closer he got to the award being announced, the more he decided he really wanted to win it.

"Guys like O.J. Simpson, Earl Campbell, Tony Dorsett—they won it, Those were guys you had watched in the pros," Marshall said.

Before the award was presented, he had a chance to talk to Simpson, who told him, "Marshall, you've got to understand. Sometimes the best player doesn't always win this award."

That proved to be an accurate prediction. The Heisman went to Miami quarterback Gino Torretta. Marshall finished second.

Even though Miami had a better team than San Diego State and had won more games, Marshall didn't believe that justified Torreta's winning the award over him.

"I felt like I should have won it," Marshall said. "I still do."

Marshall barely avoids stepping on his opponent on his way to a touchdown. (AP/Wide World Photos)

Losing out on the Heisman didn't lower the opinion of many that Marshall was ready to make the next jump in his career, moving on to the NFL. Marshall said he never really thought about it, knowing in his heart he was coming back to San Diego State for his junior year.

"I was having the time of my youthful life," he said. "I actually had some direction, with school. I figured I had a chance at football and I was happy. I wasn't really thinking about the money."

Playing against defenses that were designed to stop him, Marshall still rushed for 1,530 yards and 21 touchdowns. He also caught a career-high 47 passes. In the Heisman voting, Marshall finished fourth.

In three years, Marshall had rushed for 4,589 yards and 57 touchdowns and had caught an additional 82 passes, including five touchdowns. He had a career rushing average of 148 yards a game and topped the 100-yard mark in 23 of his 32 collegiate games. He rushed for more than 200 yards seven times and more than 300 yards twice. He scored at least one touchdown in 27 of his 32 games.

When Coach Al Luginbill and his staff were let go at the end of the season, Marshall's mind was made up. It was time to become a professional.

"Marshall Faulk and this program was a marriage made in heaven," Luginbill told *The Sporting News*. "He was the right man at the right time with the right demeanor. In 25 years of athletics I have never seen an impact like it. I don't just mean to a program, but to a community.

"He's an upbeat kid with a great personality. The normal person in the street can look at him and think, that guy could be my friend. As a result, there is no athlete in San Diego who is more popular than Marshall right now. None. Tony Gwynn? Marshall Faulk has equal status."

Marshall said if Luginbill and his assistants had not been fired, he would have returned for his senior year.

"I felt like if I was going to be learning a new system I might as well be doing it in the pros," Marshall said. "Other than maybe winning a national championship—which our program was not close to doing—there wasn't much more I could accomplish in college."

Just as he had had doubts about how well he would be able to do in college football three years earlier, Marshall was worried about the transition to the professional game. How would he do against the best football players in the world? He was ready to find out.

Marshall was stressed out the night before the NFL draft.
(Joe Robbins)

5

The Pro Game

The night before the NFL draft was a restless one for Marshall. So much of his future—monetarily as well as football success—could be determined in large part by which team selected Marshall and with what pick. It was a foregone conclusion that he would go high in the draft, but he didn't know where.

The Cincinnati Bengals owned the first pick and even though they seemed pleased with their running game, Marshall thought they might take

Marshall was surprised to be picked by the Colts.
(Joe Robbins)

him. He was only slightly surprised when the Bengals announced their top pick—defensive tackle Dan Wilkinson.

The Indianapolis Colts were picking second, and they were one team that Marshall had not had contact with during the evaluating of prospects after the end of the college season.

"I had never talked to the Colts," he said. "I didn't talk to them at the combine, and I don't think they had a representative at my workout."

Marshall's one connection with Indianapolis had been attending the combine—where college prospects work out for various NFL teams in different drills and are examined by doctors for medical reports — in February.

"It was so freaking cold I remember getting on the airplane to go back to San Diego and saying 'I'll never come back here,'" Marshall said.

Marshall was at the NFL draft in New York when he heard the words, "With the second pick, the Indianapolis Colts select Marshall Faulk, running back, San Diego State."

For a moment, Marshall didn't know what to think. He was happy, but he also knew he knew nothing about the Colts or their organization.

The organization also had to get to know Marshall. "It was a good time to be bad, if there is such a thing," said Bill Tobin, the team's director of football operations. The Colts had gone 4-12 the previous season and even though two highly regarded quarterbacks were available, Heath Shuler and Trent Dilfer, Tobin and the Colts decided to talk Marshall.

As he studied the team and got to know the personnel and the coaching staff, he found out the Colts were going to be a good fit for him. They needed running backs, and he quickly developed a good relationship with Coach Ted Marchibroda.

"He did a good job of getting the team ready to play," Marshall said. "He probably was the best coach I've had. He knew how to deal with players on a level that most coaches have a problem with. A lot of coaches can coach and be a dictator, but he's a teacher too. He knows the game, and it makes it easier to learn because you know he knows what he is talking about."

Marchibroda also was pleased with Marshall and what his addition meant to the team.

"We lacked a big play guy on offense," Marchibroda said. "A guy who can become a pressure-point player who forces the defense to focus on him and stop him before they do anything else. Marshall is that kind of guy."

Marshall was worried about having to make adjustments to the pro game, but he didn't have much problem. When the Colts took their field

Marshall finished his rookie year in the NFL with 1,282 yards and 11 touchdowns. (Joe Robbins)

against Houston for their first game of the 1994 regular season, Marshall was in the starting lineup.

Just as he had done in his high school and college debuts as well, he was ready. The 13th time he touched the ball, he gained 56 yards. The next carry went for 11 yards and a touchdown. For the game, he rushed for 143 yards and three touchdowns, one of the best inaugural games by a running back in NFL history.

He wasn't a one-game sensation either. He rushed for 104 yards the next week against Tampa Bay and also caught seven passes. Marshall had two more 100-yard games and finished his rookie year by rushing for 1,282 yards and 11 touchdowns.

"I'm not going to tell you I thought I could walk into this league and do this well right away," Marshall said at the time. "You don't have strong doubts, but you always wonder, watching these guys on TV. They look so big and strong. Can you keep up?"

Marshall found out the answer was yes. He was named the NFL Offensive Rookie of the Year and was named a starter for the AFC in the Pro Bowl. Marshall set eight Colts rookie records and tied another.

He made believers out of people around the league, including Charley Casserly, the general manager of the Washington Redskins.

"Faulk is a great player already, an elite player," Casserly told *The Sporting News*. "Is he better than (Barry) Sanders, (Thurman) Thomas or (Emmitt) Smith? You can't say he isn't, but he is going to have to prove it. But he has that kind of ability."

The highlight of his season was the trip to the Pro Bowl, where Marshall had to pinch himself to make certain he was really there.

"The first Pro Bowl is the best," he said. "I was in the same room with (John) Elway, (Drew) Bledsoe, Bruce Smith—it was like 'Man, I've watched this game on TV.' I'm about to play in this game. It was a greet feeling."

The feeling was improved by the fact Marshall played a spectacular game against the best players in the NFL, rushing for a record 180 yards, adding 27 yards on pass receptions and being named the game's MVP.

Marshall and the Colts were coming together, and they made major strides in his second season. They came within one play of winning the AFC championship and going to the Super Bowl, but a long pass attempt was unsuccessful in their attempt to beat the Steelers.

Marshall had to watch that game from the sidelines. He had to undergo knee surgery following the first playoff game at San Diego, and missed the

Although Marshall suffered several injuries, it didn't slow him down. (Brian Spurlock)

games against Kansas City and Pittsburgh. He says he would have been ready for the Super Bowl.

In the regular season, Marshall went over 1,000 yards for the second consecutive year, gaining 1,078. He also caught four more passes than the previous year, improving from 52 to 56, and made the Pro Bowl for the second consecutive season.

Despite the team's success, Marchibroda was let go as coach, a move that surprised and disappointed Marshall.

"I was upset, but that just tells you the way things are," he said.

That move was the start of a disappointing season for Marshall. The Colts made it back to the playoffs, but this time lost to Pittsburgh in the wild-card game. Marshall missed three games because of injuries and rushed for only 587 yards.

He came back stronger in 1997, however, and again topped the 1,000 yard mark with 1,054 rushing yards, enjoying four 100-yard games.

By 1998, Marshall had established himself as one of the best running backs in the league. He again produced a 1,000-yard season—his fourth in his five years in the league—by finishing the year with 1,319 yards. He also led the Colts with 86 receptions, good for 908 yards.

In the final game of the season he had a chance to become only the second player—joining Roger Craig of the 49ers—in NFL history to rush for 1,000 yards and also to have 1,000 or more yards in pass receptions in the same season. His 86 receptions did break a franchise record.

Despite his performance, the Colts stumbled to a 3-13 record, finishing last in the AFC East. They had brought in a rookie quarterback, Peyton Manning, and he had played well, but the Colts were no longer the veteran team that had come so close to making the Super Bowl only three years earlier.

"It was a frustrating year but when you get rid of a lot of key people you've got to expect that to happen," Marshall said. "There are not a lot of young teams that are playing in the Super Bowl."

During the closing weeks of the season, Marshall begin to think that maybe he didn't fit into the Colts future plans. He wanted to renegotiate the contract he had signed before his rookie season, but the team executives kept putting off meetings with his agent.

"I understand the business side of the game and I've got no problem with that," Marshall said. "It's hard, though, because you feel like you put a lot of work into something and play your heart out and then you realize you're just a toy. The team can dispose of you whenever they want.

Marshall was initially disappointed when he was traded to the Rams. (Joe Robbins)

"They use you to sell tickets—'Come see Marshall play'—but when they are ready to get rid of you it's 'Why can't Marshall convert on third-and-one?' Something like that doesn't motivate me. I stay motivated all the time. I don't need anything extra to get me up. I'm up to play football all the time."

Even though Marshall had an idea the Colts were looking to trade him, it still came as a shock when General Manager Jim Irsay called him in April 1999 to tell him he had been traded to the St. Louis Rams.

"I understand them saying what they did, because you've got to make excuses when you do something," Marshall said. "They've got to try to justify to the 60,000 people coming to their games that they are trying to win and not just taking their money.

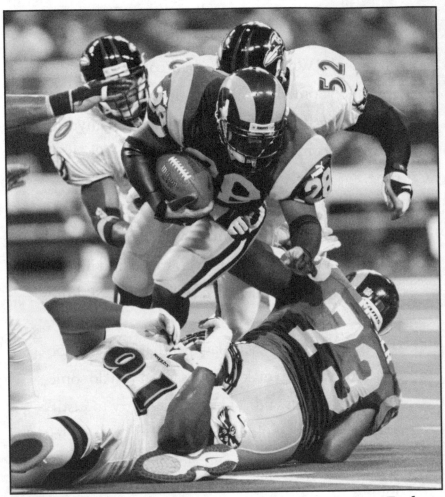

Marshall gets tripped up as he goes over Rams teammate Fred Miller. (AP/Wide World Photos)

"In three or four years they are going to know one of two things. They are going to know they did the right thing in trading me, or they didn't do the right thing. Only time will tell."

Marshall bobbles the ball during the second half of the Rams'
victory in St. Louis. (AP/Wide World Photos)

CHAPTER SIX

The Future

Marshall realized a long time ago how lucky he is to be a professional football player. He knows there have been many times when his life could have gone a different direction, and he is grateful for everything that has happened to him.

One lesson he has tried never to forget was something a former strength coach of the Colts, Tom Zupancic, said to him during his rookie season.

"He said, 'Marshall, if you ever travel down a road where there's no speed bumps, you're headed for a dead end." I've always thought about that, because it made a lot of sense. If you apply that to life, and not just to football, you can see that it's true.

"Think of all the kids who grow up with everything. They hit that dead end and they're done. When you are on that bumpy road and things are not going the way you anticipated or the way you would like for them to go, that's the way life is.

"Life is a bunch of speed bumps. If you don't get tired of going over them or don't let any of them stop you, you are going to lead a long life."

Most of Marshall's speed bumps came before he reached high school, but one person who wasn't so lucky was a future Carver High School player, Cedrick Favaroth. Cedrick was an All-State running back who was being pursued by many Division I schools when his senior season was to begin in 1998.

In a freak accident, Cedrick severed an artery in his right leg during practice and doctors were forced to amputate his leg above the knee.

Marshall found out about the accident from a former teacher and his brother. In November, he flew Cedrick, Cedrick's brother and sister-in-law to Indianapolis. They met, ate dinner and Cedrick and his relatives were Marshall's guests on the sideline for the Colts game against the New York Jets.

"I didn't know how to approach him or what to say to him," Marshall said. "I didn't know how he was going to react. I didn't know if I should talk about football or not. When I met him, the first thing he said was how he couldn't wait to get his prothesis to see if he could go out and play football again. It was just amazing. He has such a great attitude. I know I would have been devastated."

Marshall tries to fend off Atlanta Falcons' Chuck Smith.
(AP/Wide World Photos)

Marshall still talks with Cedrick on occasion and said he will most likely bring him to a game in St. Louis during the 1999 season.

Every time he meets someone like Cedrick, or sees other people who never were able to see their dreams come true, Marshall knows how truly lucky and fortunate he has been.

"I can remember almost every game I've played," Marshall said. "Some people never get that chance. The guys playing in the Arena League and the World League; they are out there because they hope to get a shot at the NFL. Playing in the NFL is a job, but it is up to you to make it fun. That's what I've tried to do."

Marshall isn't sure how many more years he hopes to play, but he would like to try to move into broadcasting when his playing career is over.

"I want to play as long as I can because I enjoy the game," he said. "The minute I can't go to prac-

Marshall is held to a two-yard gain by Chicago Bears' Barry Minter. (AP/Wide World Photos)

tice and enjoy practice then I know I'm not going to want to play the game. You can't go out on Sunday and perform your best if you don't do well in practice. When I can't get any better than I'm done."

Marshall also hopes to keep working on his golf game with the same intensity. Three years ago, he took up the sport because he was so embarrassed when he couldn't hit the ball at Eric Dickerson's celebrity tournament.

"I work at golf with the same intensity I do football because it's just as challenging," Marshall said. "Three years ago I couldn't hit the ball and I was just devastated."

It's not surprising that Marshall is a much better golfer now. It was another challenge—and Marshall has been overcoming challenges his entire life. He's not about to stop now.

Marshall Faulk Quick Facts

Name: Marshall William Faulk

Team: St. Louis Rams

Number: 28

Height/Weight: 5' 10"/208 lbs.

Birthdate: February 26, 1973

Hometown: New Orleans, Louisiana

Years in the League: 5

Drafted: First Round (2nd overall)

College: San Diego State

1998 Highlight: Had best season of career by setting Colts single-season record and led the NFL with 2,227 total yards from scrimmage, the sixth-highest total in league history, accounting for 43.5 percent of Colts yards.

Statistical Highlight: The only player in the NFL with at least 900 yards rushing and 324 attempts with six touchdowns.

Little known for: His major in college was Public Administration.

Marshall Faulk's NFL Statistics

Career Rushing

Year	Rush Yds.	Rush Avg.	TD
1994	1,282	4.1	11
1995	1,078	3.7	11
1996	587	3.0	7
1997	1,054	4.0	7
1998	1,319	4.1	6
1999	369	5.1	1
Totals	5,689	3.9	43
Playoff	41	4.1	0

Career Receiving

Year	Rec. Yds.	Rec. Avg.	TD
1994	522	10.0	1
1995	475	8.5	3
1996	428	7.6	0
1997	471	10.0	1
1998	908	10.6	4
1999	226	10.3	1
Totals	3030	9.5	10
Playoff	10	3.3	0

Career Scoring

Year	Rush TD	Rec. TD
1994	11	1
1995	11	3
1996	7	0
1997	7	1
1998	6	4
1999	1	1
Totals	43	10
Playoffs	0	0

1998 Rushing

Date	Opp	Att	Yds	Avg	TD	LG
09/06/98	Mia	24	56	2.3	0	11
09/13/98	@NE	29	127	4.4	0	13
09/20/98	@NYA	21	91	4.3	0	16
09/27/98	MO	27	61	2.3	0	13
10/04/98	SD	25	50	2.0	0	13
10/11/98	Buf	18	93	5.2	0	40
10/18/98	@SF	17	103	6.1	1	65
11/01/98	NE	11	22	2.0	0	5
11/08/98	@Mia	21	88	4.2	1	12
11/15/98	NYA	20	69	3.5	0	11
11/22/98	@Buf	18	85	4.7	0	17
11/29/98	@Bal	17	192	11.3	1	68
12/06/98	@Atl	19	76	4.0	1	13
12/13/98	Cin	26	115	4.4	2	24
12/20/98	@Sea	13	19	1.5	0	13
12/27/98	Car	18	72	4.0	0	11
TOTAL		324	1,319	4.1	6	68

1998 Receiving

Date	Rec	Yds	Avg	TD	LG
09/06/98	4	49	12.3	0	15
09/13/98	7	60	8.6	0	22
09/20/98	2	7	3.5	0	7
09/27/98	6	128	21.3	1	78
10/04/98	4	44	11.0	1	19
10/11/98	6	80	13.3	0	26
10/18/98	4	36	9.0	0	18
11/01/98	9	119	13.2	0	24
11/08/98	4	16	4.0	0	8
11/15/98	8	70	8.8	0	18
11/22/98	8	102	12.8	0	25
11/29/98	7	75	10.7	1	34
12/06/98	7	37	5.3	1	11
12/13/98	2	39	19.5	0	23
12/20/98	4	16	4.0	0	11
12/27/98	4	30	7.5	0	15
TOTAL	86	908	10.6	4	78

Baseball Superstar Series Titles

Collect Them All!

_____ Mark McGwire: Mac Attack!

_____ #1 *Derek Jeter: The Yankee Kid*

_____ #2 *Ken Griffey Jr.: The Home Run Kid*

_____ #3 *Randy Johnson: Arizona Heat!*

_____ #4 *Sammy Sosa: Slammin' Sammy*

_____ #5 *Bernie Williams: Quiet Superstar*

_____ #6 *Omar Vizquel: The Man with the Golden Glove*

_____ #7 *Mo Vaughn: Angel on a Mission*

_____ #8 *Pedro Martinez: Throwing Strikes*

_____ #9 *Juan Gonzalez: Juan Gone!*

_____ #10 *Tony Gwynn: Mr. Padre*

_____ #11 *Kevin Brown: Kevin with a "K"*

_____ #12 *Mike Piazza: Mike and the Mets*

_____ #13 *Larry Walker: Canadian Rocky*

_____ #14 *Nomar Garciaparra: High 5!*

_____ #15 *Sandy and Roberto Alomar: Baseball Brothers*

_____ #16 *Mark Grace: Winning with Grace*

_____ #17 *Curt Schilling: Phillie Phire!*

_____ #18 *Alex Rodriguez: A+ Shortstop*

_____ #19 *Roger Clemens: Rocket!*

Only $4.95 per book!

Football Superstar Series Titles
Collect Them All!

____ #1 *Ed McCaffrey: Catching a Star*

____ #3 *Peyton Manning: Passing Legacy*

____ #4 *Jake Plummer: Comeback Cardinal*

____ #5 *Mark Brunell: Super Southpaw*

____ #6 *Drew Bledsoe: Patriot Rifle*

____ #7 *Junior Seau: Overcoming the Odds*

____ #8 *Marshall Faulk: Rushing to Glory*

Only $4.95 per book!

Basketball Superstar Series Titles

Collect Them All!

_____ #1 *Kobe Bryant: The Hollywood Kid*

_____ #2 *Keith Van Horn: Nothing But Net*

_____ #3 *Antoine Walker: Kentucky Celtic*

_____ #4 *Kevin Garnett: Scratching the Surface*

_____ #5 *Tim Duncan: Slam Duncan*

_____ #6 *Reggie Miller: From Downtown*

_____ #7 *Jason Kidd: Rising Sun*

_____ #8 *Vince Carter: Air Canada*

Only $4.95 per book!

Hockey Superstar Series Titles
Collect Them All!

___ #1 *John LeClair: Flying High*

___ #2 *Mike Richter: Gotham Goalie*

___ #3 *Paul Kariya: Maine Man*

___ #4 *Dominik Hasek: The Dominator*

___ #5 *Jaromir Jagr: Czechmate*

___ #6 *Martin Brodeur: Picture Perfect*

___ #8 *Ray Bourque: Bruins Legend*

Only $4.95 per book!